VICTOR WEMBANYAMA

BASKETBALL SUPERSTAR

BY ANTHONY K. HEWSON

Copyright © 2025 by Press Room Editions. All rights reserved. No part of this book may be used or reproduced in any manner whatsoever, including internet usage, without written permission from the copyright owner, except in the case of brief quotations embodied in critical articles and reviews.

Book design by Jake Nordby
Cover design by Jake Nordby

Photographs ©: Abbie Parr/AP Images, cover, 1; Michel Euler/AP Images, 4–5, 7; Thearon W. Henderson/Getty Images Sport/Getty Images, 8–9; Anthony Dibon/Icon Sport/Getty Images, 10; Loic Baratoux/Abaca/Sipa USA/AP Images, 13; Sonia Canada/Getty Images Sport/Getty Images, 15; Cordon Press/Sipa USA/AP Images, 16; Bob Edme/AP Images, 19; Christian Liewig/Corbis Sport/Getty Images, 21; Brian Rothmuller/Icon Sportswire/AP Images, 22, 30; Christian Petersen/Getty Images Sport/Getty Images, 25; Steph Chambers/Getty Images Sport/Getty Images, 26; Red Line Editorial, 29

Press Box Books, an imprint of Press Room Editions, Inc.

ISBN
978-1-63494-934-7 (library bound)
978-1-63494-939-2 (paperback)
978-1-63494-948-4 (epub)
978-1-63494-944-6 (hosted ebook)

Library of Congress Control Number: 2024939611

Distributed by North Star Editions, Inc.
2297 Waters Drive
Mendota Heights, MN 55120
www.northstareditions.com

Printed in the United States of America
082024

About the Author

Anthony K. Hewson is a freelance writer originally from San Diego. He and his wife now live in San Francisco with their two dogs.

TABLE OF CONTENTS

CHAPTER 1
Reaching for the Win 5

SPECIAL FEATURE
Look Out Above 8

CHAPTER 2
Advanced for His Age 11

CHAPTER 3
Standing Tall 17

CHAPTER 4
Living Up to the Hype 23

Timeline • 28
At a Glance • 30
Glossary • 31
To Learn More • 32
Index • 32

1 REACHING FOR THE WIN

Victor Wembanyama and his team were running out of time. The clock ticked under 20 seconds to play. Two of France's best teams were battling in a game during the 2022–23 season. Wembanyama's Metropolitans 92 trailed ASVEL 83–82.

ASVEL had a chance to put the game away. The 7-foot-4 (224 cm) Wembanyama set himself under the basket on defense. An open ASVEL shooter received a pass in the corner. In a flash, Wembanyama

Victor Wembanyama contests a shot against ASVEL in a 2023 game.

darted out to the shooter. He lifted his long arm to disrupt the shot. The ball clanged off the rim. The Metropolitans were still alive.

The clock ticked under 10 seconds. Metropolitans guard Tremont Waters drove to the basket. He dashed around a defender and put up a shot. The ball hit the side of the rim. A follow-up shot bounced off the glass. It looked like the Metropolitans were going to run out of time. However, Wembanyama wouldn't give up.

The center camped out in the paint. He jumped over a defender. Then he snatched the ball with his

GLOBAL AUDIENCE

Victor Wembanyama had plenty of fans in his native France. By 2022, he also had some in North America. Analysts expected Wembanyama to enter the 2023 National Basketball Association (NBA) Draft. So, the NBA showed Metropolitans games online. That let many fans get their first glimpse of Wembanyama.

Wembanyama fires up the crowd after leading the Metropolitans to a win over ASVEL.

long arms. In the same motion, he dunked the ball powerfully through the hoop to give his team the lead.

Metropolitans fans roared in celebration. They had seen Wembanyama's heroics regularly by now. Watching the French phenom never got old, though. Soon the rest of the world would see Wembanyama's talent on full display.

LOOK OUT ABOVE

Shooters have to be careful around Wembanyama. His arms stretch out nearly 8 feet (244 cm) wide. When he jumps, it makes shooting over him nearly impossible.

2 ADVANCED FOR HIS AGE

Victor Wembanyama was born on January 4, 2004. He grew up in Le Chesnay, a suburb of Paris, France. From a young age, Victor seemed destined to be a basketball player. His mother, Elodie, had played and coached basketball for years. His grandparents had played, too.

Victor's family provided him with the height he needed to be a star. Elodie stood 6-foot-3 (191 cm). His father, Felix, was 6-foot-6 (198 cm). Felix didn't play basketball. But he ran track.

Victor Wembanyama first started playing professional basketball when he was 15.

A BASKETBALL FAMILY

Victor grew up with an older sister and a younger brother. They all played basketball. Victor's sister, Eve, played pro basketball in Europe. She also played on France's youth 3-on-3 national team. Victor's brother, Oscar, didn't play basketball until he was 14. His first sport was handball. But he quickly picked up hoops. By 16, Oscar caught the attention of pro scouts.

Growing up near Paris, the game of basketball surrounded Victor. However, his family never pushed him into playing only one sport. As a kid, he tried judo. Victor also excelled at soccer. With his height, he usually played goalkeeper. Basketball eventually won out, though.

Victor stood 5-foot-10 (178 cm) by the age of nine. His height quickly caught the attention of scouts.

In 2013, a coach for Nanterre 92, a French basketball club, mistook Victor for a coach of another team. Once the coach saw Victor play, he wanted Victor to join Nanterre right away.

Victor Wembanyama handles the ball during a 2021 game with Nanterre 92.

Victor started playing for Nanterre when he was 10. Because of his height and skills, he usually competed on older teams. At the age of 13, Victor played on a team for 15-year-olds. He impressed coaches with his confidence and skills at such a young age. By this point, Victor had grown to 6-foot-6 (198 cm). But he was more than just tall. He could shoot, defend, and run as well as any player.

French basketball clubs have both youth teams and professional teams. At 14, Victor seemed ready for the pros. That year, he played in a tournament for Barcelona. Few European teams were as successful as the Spanish club. Barcelona wanted Victor to join its pro team. Nanterre's pro team couldn't compare to the Spanish powerhouse. Playing for Barcelona would have been a huge step in Victor's career. However, Victor decided to stay with Nanterre. He knew the team's coaches well. He believed they would challenge him and make him a better player.

At 15, Victor began his pro career with Nanterre. His family and coaches loved that

Victor Wembanyama played professionally in France for four years.

Victor had stayed close to home. Soon, Nanterre fans would be thrilled by Victor's choice as well.

3 STANDING TALL

Veteran basketball player Keith Hornsby remembers the first time he played against Victor Wembanyama. As Hornsby looked to shoot, a 17-year-old Victor stood far away. Hornsby began his shooting motion. Then he saw a long arm appear out of nowhere. Hornsby had no time to react. Victor used his incredible reach and excellent speed to block the shot.

Victor quickly showed that he belonged in the pros. His talent had

Victor Wembanyama averaged 12.8 points per game during his pro career in France.

STUDENT ATHLETE

Turning pro didn't mean Victor had to stop going to school. He attended high school while also playing for Nanterre. In his spare time, he enjoyed making art and listening to classical music. Victor taught himself English by watching TV shows. He learned the language to prepare for the NBA.

always been obvious. However, coaches worried about how his body would hold up. Taller players often have problems with injuries. Victor was also very thin. He needed to develop more strength to handle tougher leagues.

Victor's first injury setback came during the 2020-21 season. A broken leg kept him out for two and a half months. But when he did play, he impressed. Victor won the French league's Rising Star award. That honor is for the best player under 22 years old.

The summer of 2021 proved to be an important time in Victor's career. He decided

Victor Wembanyama first played for France's senior national team in 2022.

to change teams. He left Nanterre to play for ASVEL. His new team played in Villeurbanne, France. For the first time, Victor moved away from home.

That summer, Victor also played for France in the Under-19 Basketball World Cup.

Victor was only 17 years old. That meant he was facing players who were more than a year older. Some of them had the potential to play in the NBA. Victor didn't struggle against them, though. He led France all the way to the final.

France faced the United States in the final. The Americans had dominated the tournament so far. And they had their own 7-foot-1 (216 cm) star in Chet Holmgren. The two future NBA players battled in a close game. Holmgren led the United States to a win. But Victor showed he could play with the world's best. He was named to the all-tournament team.

Victor got off to a rough start with ASVEL. Injuries slowed him down again. However, he performed well in the games he did play. And he won the Rising Star award for the second time. After the season, he chose to go back

In his one year with Metropolitans 92, Victor Wembanyama averaged 21.6 points and 10.4 rebounds per game.

home. Victor joined Metropolitans 92, a team near Paris. He believed the coaches there could better prepare him for the NBA. And NBA teams were watching him closely. Scouts went to all his games. Meanwhile, fans from all over the world were also watching the future NBA superstar.

4 LIVING UP TO THE HYPE

By 2023, no one doubted that Victor Wembanyama would be the top pick in the NBA Draft. The only question was which team would get to take him. In the NBA, having a bad record gives teams a better chance at earning a high draft pick. The league warned teams not to intentionally lose games so that they'd get the first pick. That was how much teams wanted Wembanyama.

The San Antonio Spurs ended up with the top pick. To nobody's surprise, they

Wembanyama averaged 10.6 rebounds per game during his rookie season in the NBA.

drafted Wembanyama. Fans were eager to see him play. In July, a sold-out crowd of 19,000 came to see him in an NBA Summer League game. A Summer League game hadn't sold out in years. Those games aren't even official NBA games. They're just for rookies and players trying to make a team.

In October, Wembanyama made his NBA regular-season debut. He scored 15 points. Nine of them came from three-point range. His defense stood out the most, though. Right away, opposing players avoided shooting against him.

Wembanyama quickly improved. In his fifth game, he put on a show. The Spurs had raced out to a 27-point lead against the

Wembanyama scored 30 or more points in 11 different games during his rookie year.

Wembanyama (1) led the NBA in blocks during the 2023-24 season.

Phoenix Suns. But with 4:21 to go, the Suns tied the game. Teams often turn to veteran players in clutch moments. However, the Spurs relied on Wembanyama to close out the game. He already had 28 points. Then he scored 10 of the final 12 to seal the win.

The big nights kept on coming. In February, he put up a rare five-by-five. That's when a player records at least five points, rebounds, assists, blocks, and steals. Wembanyama became the youngest player to ever record a five-by-five. Throughout his rookie season, Wembanyama thrived on both ends of the court. NBA fans had never seen any player like him before.

San Antonio didn't have a great record during the 2023-24 season. But Wembanyama had lived up to his huge pre-draft hype. Spurs fans couldn't wait to see their superstar play for years to come.

WEMBY VS. CHET

Victor Wembanyama often got compared to Oklahoma City Thunder player Chet Holmgren. Both players were tall and thin. They also had similar skills. Both players were rookies in 2023-24. The Thunder won three games against the Spurs that year. But Wembanyama won the NBA Rookie of the Year Award.

TIMELINE

1. **Le Chesnay, France (January 4, 2004)**
   Victor Wembanyama is born.

2. **Nanterre, France (2019)**
   Victor begins his pro career with Nanterre 92.

3. **Riga, Latvia (July 11, 2021)**
   Victor leads France to the final of the Under-19 Basketball World Cup.

4. **Brooklyn, New York (June 22, 2023)**
   The San Antonio Spurs select Wembanyama with the first pick in the NBA Draft.

5. **San Antonio, Texas (October 25, 2023)**
   Wembanyama makes his NBA debut, scoring 15 points in a loss to the Dallas Mavericks.

6. **Los Angeles, California (February 23, 2024)**
   Wembanyama becomes the youngest player to record a five-by-five, posting 27 points, 10 rebounds, 8 assists, 5 blocks, and 5 steals.

7. **San Antonio, Texas (March 29, 2024)**
   Wembanyama scores a career-high 40 points in a win against the New York Knicks.

8. **San Antonio, Texas (May 11, 2024)**
   The Spurs present the 2024 NBA Rookie of the Year Award to Wembanyama.

MAP

AT A GLANCE

Birth date: January 4, 2004

Birthplace: Le Chesnay, France

Position: Center

Shoots: Right

Size: 7-foot-4 (224 cm), 209 pounds (95 kg)

NBA team: San Antonio Spurs (2023-)

Previous teams: Nanterre 92 (2019-21), ASVEL (2021-22), Metropolitans 92 (2022-23)

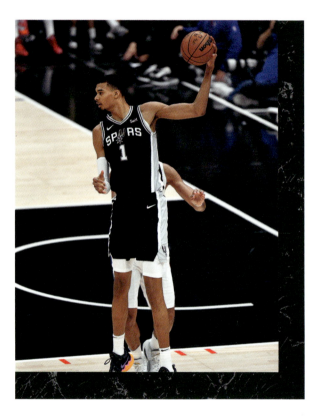

Major awards: LNB Young Player of the Year (2021-23), LNB MVP (2023), NBA Rookie of the Year (2024)

Accurate through the 2023-24 season.

GLOSSARY

clutch
A difficult situation when the outcome of the game is in question.

debut
First appearance.

draft
An event that allows teams to choose new players coming into the league.

paint
The area between the basket and the free-throw line.

phenom
A person who is extremely talented at a young age.

professional
Having to do with people who are paid to do something as a job.

rookies
First-year players.

scouts
People who look for talented young players.

setback
A difficult moment that stops progress.

veteran
A player who has spent several years in a league.

TO LEARN MORE

Books

Goldstein, Margaret J. *Meet Victor Wembanyama: San Antonio Spurs Superstar.* Minneapolis: Lerner Publications, 2025.

Hanlon, Luke. *Everything Basketball.* Minneapolis: Abdo Publishing, 2024.

Moussavi, Sam, and John Willis. *San Antonio Spurs.* New York: Lightbox Learning, 2023.

More Information

To learn more about Victor Wembanyama, go to **pressboxbooks.com/AllAccess.**

These links are routinely monitored and updated to provide the most current information available.

INDEX

ASVEL, 5, 19–20

Barcelona, 14

France national team, 19–20

Holmgren, Chet, 20, 27

Hornsby, Keith, 17

Metropolitans 92, 5–7, 21

Nanterre 92, 12–15, 18–19

NBA Draft, 6, 23

Oklahoma City Thunder, 27

Phoenix Suns, 26

Rising Star award, 18, 20

Rookie of the Year Award, 27

Summer League, 24

Under-19 Basketball World Cup, 19–20

Waters, Tremont, 6